First published in Great Britain in 2005
Michael O'Mara Books Limited,
9 Lion Yard, Tremadoc Road,
London, SW4 7NQ, UK
www.mombooks.com

Text and illustrations © 2005 by Tim Collins

Edited by Philippa Wingate
Designed by Zoe Quayle

A CIP catalogue record for this book
is available from the British Library.

ISBN 1-84317-100-7

1 3 5 7 9 10 8 6 4 2
Printed and bound in Great Britain
by Cox & Wyman, Reading, Berks

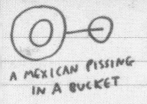
A MEXICAN PISSING IN A BUCKET

School: Rules

by Tim Collins

INTRODUCTION

When we start school, we're told there'll be no running in the corridors, no chewing gum in class, and that we should always raise our hands before answering a question.

These, we're told, are the school rules.

But the rules we really follow are different:

- Never tell anyone it's your birthday, in case they flush your head down the toilet.
- Always draw tits and knobs on your textbooks.
- Always ask another pupil to pull your finger before you fart.
- Never, under any circumstances, get caught reading a book instead of playing British Bulldog at lunchtime.

Of course, we never see these rules written down. We just kind of pick them up, to make sure that we're not the ones who get given wedgies and deadlegs by the hard kids.

The real rules of school might help bring back a few memories. After all, who doesn't still cheer when the fire alarm goes off, or sing 'Listen to this, too good to miss' when they feel a fart coming.

DAVE
IS GAY
BY
RICK

RULE NO.1

You must always make fun of people who are different from you.

RULE NO.2

If you are ever getting picked on for being fat, geeky or poor, you must find someone who is fatter, geekier or poorer than you, and get everyone to pick on them instead.

RULE NO.3

Never, under any circumstances, sit next to the class spazmo.

Ganja

RULE NO.4

If one of your friends sits next to the class spazmo, tell everyone that he or she has caught bum disease off the spazmo.

Rule No.5

If a teacher forces you to sit next to the class spazmo, and there's no way you can get out of it, create a protective barrier around yourself using textbooks, exercise books and A4 ring binders.

Rule No.6

If a pupil you hate tries to talk to you when you're with your gang, ask them if it's true that they can't wipe their own arse and that their mum has to do it for them.

Rule No.7

Always say 'No returns' after you hit someone, to ensure that they can't hit you back.

Rule No.8

If someone says 'No returns' to you, you should hit them back anyway.

RULE NO.9

Never sit down on a chair without checking it first for drawing pins, chewing gum, glue or greenies.

RULE NO.10

If the class spazmo sits in front of you, spend the whole lesson spitting on their back.

RULE NO.11

If someone makes up a lie about you, like you got arrested for bumming a cat, don't go around denying it. You will just look guilty.

RULE NO.12

Textbooks are school property, and should be treated as such. Draw knobs and tits on all the pictures, black out people's teeth, and draw clouds of fart coming out of their arses.

RULE NO.13

Defacing Biology textbooks is more difficult, as some of the pictures are already quite rude. Try drawing eyes on the sperm, or turning a diagram of the female reproductive organs into a smiley face, using the ovaries as eyes.

RULE NO. 14

You must recite the following poem:

My friend Billy

Had a ten-foot willy

And he showed it to the girl next door

She thought it was a snake

So she hit it with a rake

And now it's only five foot four

RULE NO.15

When farting, let off into your hand and throw it at someone.

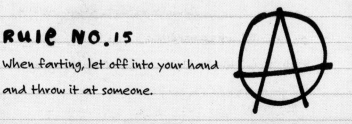

Rule No.16

When a thick pupil gets a question wrong, make a spastic noise and flop your arms around.

Rule No.17

Tell the thickest kid in your class that the word 'gullible' has been taken out of the dictionary.

Rule No.18

Always tease the kid in your class who is last to grow pubes, and call them 'Baldy'. You should continue to tease them about it long after they've actually grown pubes.

Rule No.19

When you fart, you should do an impression of Jilly Goolden from BBC TV's 'Food and Drink', and say, 'Well, it's a cheeky little number, I'm getting eggs, I'm getting beef, I'm getting onions...'

Compulsory Games

- Who can leave the highest footmark on the wall?

- Who can flick poo at the class spazmo with a stick?

- Who can kick a football over the annex roof?

- Who can climb up on the annex roof to get the football off it?

- Take turns with a friend to punch each other in the stomach. The loser is the person who gives up first.

- Bend someone's fingers back and see how long they can stand it before they squeal 'Mercy'.

- Throw 10p pieces against a wall. The person whose coin lands nearest to the wall wins all the money.

- Who can piss highest in the urinal?

GRAHAM'S MUM

RULE NO.20

After farting, you should bend down to where your arse was, sniff it, and give it a mark out of 10.

RULE NO.21

Call someone a geek if they wear glasses, or braces, if they constantly correct the teachers, or if they've memorized Pi to 20 decimal places.

RULE NO.22

After snotting up, you should either flob your greenie out of the top-floor window on to the stairwell banister, or on to an empty chair.

Rule No.23

You must sing the following song on the school coach:

The driver smells of piss

The driver smells of piss

Eye-i-end-i-o

The driver smells of piss

Rule No.24

If you sneak a bottle of Thunderbird on to the school coach, only share it with the kids who were cool enough to get a seat on the back row.

Rule No.25

If the coach goes past any weirdos, you should point at them and shout at the class spazmo, 'There's your dad, wave to him.'

Andy is a Joey

Rule No.26

When on a trip, you're an ambassador for your school. Always wait until the gift-shop clerk's back is turned before you nick a dinosaur ruler, glittery stickers or a love-heart rubber.

Rule No.27

When the school coach goes through the countryside, you should accuse your friend of letting off when the smell of cow shit wafts in through the windows.

Rule No.28

You must throw yourself out of your seat if the coach goes over a speed bump, and get really excited if the coach goes into a tunnel.

RULE NO.29

Pupils who are too poor to go on the school trip must spend all day reading, while a supply teacher looks after them. When they get back, everyone who went on the trip must tell the poor kids it was brilliant, even if it was just to the Science Museum.

RULE NO.30

If the school trip is to a museum, you should spend the whole time smoking in the cafeteria.

S.W.A.L.K

RULE NO.31

If you are sitting next to a pupil you hate in the lunch hall, unscrew the salt cellar before they use it, so their food gets covered in salt.

RULE NO.32

If one of your friends gets some Doc Martens, you should stamp on their feet to see if they've got steel toecaps. It's a good idea to ask them if they collect stamps before doing this.

RULE NO.33

If a girl comes in wearing Kickers or Doc Martens, tell her she's wearing lesbian boots.

RULE NO.34

If a thick kid tries to hang around with you, dare him to pick up a dog shit. If he actually does it, tell everyone that he eats dog shit for his dinner.

RULE NO.35

You must sing the following song:

> I was walking down the lane
>
> When I felt a funny pain

Diarrhoea

Diarrhoea

So I went behind a bush

And it came out in a rush

Diarrhoea

Diarrhoea

RULE NO.36

Although the newsagents won't let you look at porno mags, you might be able to get your cheapies from the following things: video magazines with adverts for pornos in, photography magazines with articles on how to take glamour photos, the 'National Geographic', pin-ups on the walls of builders' portacabins and boards of KP nuts with pictures of naked ladies on.

RULE NO.37

If two boys from your class hang around together all the time, you must call them the Bum Chums.

RULE NO.38

You are not allowed to leave your chair during a lesson, unless someone does a fart that's so bad everyone has to run to the other side of the classroom and pull their jumpers up over their noses.

RULE NO.39

If you see a piece of cat poo on the ground, you should shout 'Catch it!' and throw it at your friend. Then say, 'I told you it was cat shit.'

RULE NO.40

By the fourth year, all girls must claim that they're virgins and all boys must deny being virgins, meaning that either all the boys are shagging girls at other schools, or bumming each other.

RULE NO.41

If you hear that the headmaster is doing emergency bag inspections to find out who has the fluorescent graffiti markers, put all your porno mags into the class spazmo's bag.

RULE NO.42

Say 'Gays are deaf' really quietly to your friend. If he says 'What?' explain that this means he's gay.

RULE NO.43

In every school there should be one really strict teacher that all the other teachers threaten to fetch when they can't control the class.

RULE NO.44

If one of your friends has bad breath, tell everyone they've been eating dog food because that's all their mum can afford to buy from Tesco's.

RULE NO.45

If a supply teacher takes the class, swap names with another pupil. Then spend the lesson behaving so badly, that the other pupil's name gets taken down and they get in trouble with the headmistress.

RULE NO.46

Get someone from the class to pretend to the supply teacher that you've got Tourette's syndrome, and that you have to shout 'Fuck' in a high-pitched voice every five minutes.

RULE NO.47

You must recite the following poem:

> Donald Duck did a muck
>
> On the kitchen floor
>
> When his mum cleaned it up
>
> Donald did some more

The Most Exciting
School Days

- The day a dog runs into the playground.

- The day the headmaster calls an emergency assembly to find out who did a shit in the PE cupboard.

- The day someone brings in a porno mag they've found.

- The day the teacher starts crying in class.

- The day a pigeon flies into the classroom.

- The day everyone watches some dogs shagging each other in front of the school railings.

- The day someone kicks a ball out of the school grounds, and it dents a car bonnet.

- The day a policeman comes into assembly and shows you a gory road-safety video.

- The day the school bully's parents have to come in and talk to the headmaster.

- The day someone shits in the swimming pool.

- The day the usually calm teacher snaps and has a Benny in class.

- The day pigeon shit lands on someone's head.
- The day after something really exciting has happened on TV, like the 'Blue Peter' garden getting vandalised, or someone asking Five Star why they're 'so fucking crap' on 'Going Live'.
- The day someone falls into some dog poo.
- The Monday after some ex-pupils have vandalized the school during the weekend.

Mark's trainers

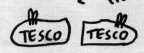

RULE NO.48

You must spend every lesson spouting reasons why you'll never need to know what's being taught. In Maths, you should say that there's no point because calculators have been invented, and in German, say that there's no point because you're never going to go to Germany for your holidays.

Rule No.49

Every fifth-year girl must think she is too mature to go out with boys from school. She must get an older boyfriend who picks her up outside the school gates in his car.

Rule No.50

If you spot two pupils having an argument, stand near them and chant, 'Fight!' If they back down, spread the rumour that they're going to have the fight in the playing fields after school, and spend the rest of the day stirring it up between them.

Rule No.51

When bunking off school, you should go down to the local shopping precinct and spit on people's heads from the balcony, ride a shopping trolley from the supermarket car park down to the canal, or go to a high-rise block and press all the buzzers at once.

RULE NO.52

If the truancy officer catches you, give him the name of the pupil you hate.

RULE NO.53

If you go to a private school and a pupil from a comprehensive walks past your playground, shout 'Pikey', 'Scabby', 'Gyppo' or 'Welfare Sponger' at them.

RULE NO.54

If you go to a comprehensive school and a pupil from a private school walks past your playground, you must put on a posh voice and shout, 'Oh, I say', 'Jolly hockey sticks' or 'Spiffing' at them.

RULE NO.55

Do not try and snap your fingers in a cool, homeboy way if you don't know how to make the clicking noise. You'll just look spastic.

Rule No.56

You must not talk to any new pupils who join the school, because they've got the lurgy. Anyone who tries to make friends with them will catch it.

smoke weed

Rule No.57

All poor kids must stay at home on No Uniform Day.

Rule No.58

If any poor kids do come in on No Uniform Day, you should sing, 'Let's go down to Tesco's, Where (name of poor kid) gets their best clothes.'

Rule No.59

If your mate comes in on No Uniform Day wearing a LeShark t-shirt instead of a LaCoste one, catalogue jeans instead of Levis, St Michael slacks instead of Farahs or market trainers instead of Nikes, give them a dead leg.

Rule No.60

You must recite the following poem:

Ee by gum

Can your belly touch your bum?

Do your balls hang low?

Do they dangle to and fro?

Can you tie them in a knot?

Can you tie them in a bow?

Rule No.61

If someone tries to jinx you for saying a word at the same time as them, pretend you jinxed them first, and give them a dead arm.

Rule No.62

You should cough or sneeze all over your lunch before eating it, so none of your mates can steal any. Also, spit into any soft drinks you buy.

RULE NO. 63

If you want to flick the Vs at someone, but are scared of getting caught by the teacher, you should put your hand up against your face and pretend to be leaning on it.

RULE NO. 64

Tell everyone that a friend of a friend was getting a blowjob off a girl, when his knob got stuck in her braces. They had to go to hospital in an ambulance, with her still kneeling down in front of him.

RULE NO. 65

If one of your teachers does an 'Awareness-Raising' assembly about handicapped people, you should put your hand up at the end and ask if people who wear glasses count as handicapped. You should then look round at the speccy kid in your class and laugh.

RULE NO.66

All boys must stick one of their fingers out of their fly, wiggle it and say, 'Look girls, it's my willy.'

RULE NO.67

If the girl you fancy finally lets you have a go on her, you should give her a hickie, grab one of her tits and fiddle with her bra strap for a bit before giving up. Then ram your tongue into her mouth, while occasionally clacking your teeth against hers.

RULE NO.68

You must tell the gullible kids that you'll die if you drink Coke and eat Space Dust at the same time, that the secret ingredient in chewing gum is spiders' eggs, and that KFC breed chickens with no beaks, no feet and no feathers.

RULE NO.69

You must superglue a 10p piece to the floor, and shout, 'Gyppo', 'Pikey' or 'Scabby Bastard' at anyone who tries to pick it up.

RULE NO.70

'Jingle Bells' must sung in the following way:

Jingle Bells

Batman smells

Robin flew away

Kojak lost his lollypop

And found a Milky Way

RULE NO.71

You must try and convince all foreign exchange students that 'shit' is English for 'please' and 'fuck off' is English for 'thanks'.

RULE NO.72

If someone asks you if you've seen a girl's fanny, answer yes, even though the closest you've got was when you joined your laced fingers with your friend and looked inside, or when the class weirdo stuck his willy between his legs in the showers.

☆ RULE NO.73

You should invent a secret code to talk to your friends in, so you can be rude about people even when they're right next to you.

← John's dad = David Hasselhoff

RULE NO.74

You should ask the pupil you hate if it's true his mum's a prostitute who hangs around outside the 50p shop, next to the sign that reads, 'No need to ask – everything you see is 50p'.

Things You Must Do
When The Teacher Leaves
The Class Unattended

- Throw the class boffin's scientific calculator around the classroom, so he has to run after it.

- Go to the front of the class, pretend to be a teacher, and say, "Right class, today's lesson is called Why is Robert so gay?'

- Try and get from one side of the classroom to the other without touching the floor.

- Steal the teacher's crib sheet and shout out all the questions when he/she gets back in the room.

- Add the names of all the kids you hate to the teacher's detention list.

- Flick the light switch on and off and have a disco.

- Get the keys to the stockroom out of the teacher's desk, and lock the class spazmo in it.

- Run your fingernails down the blackboard.

- Draw a huge cock on the blackboard and write, 'Rub me off' next to it.

RULE NO.75

If you do a fart that's so bad even you don't enjoy sniffing it, warn your friends about it so you can all run away and leave it for someone else to walk into.

RULE NO.76

Anyone who goes to a Chess, Music, or Drama club after school is a faggot.

RULE NO.77

If a pupil you hate asks if they can borrow one of your felt tips, you should give them the pink one, and say, 'You can have the gay pen.'

RULE NO.78

If you are eating lunch next to a pupil with a massive spot, you should stick a bit of sweetcorn, a chunk of diced carrot or a pea in the same place on your face and say, 'Look! This is you.'

RULE NO.79

If the class bell-end asks you for a chew from your 10p mix, you should hold it out as if to give it to him, but then say, 'Psyche' and take it away at the last minute. Repeat this until he goes away.

RULE NO.80

If your friend talks to a girl, run up to him and do a sex mime by making a fist with your left hand and shoving the index finger of your right hand into it.

RULE NO.81

If you've got a massive burp coming, you should lean over one of the girls in your class and retch like you're going to be sick before you let it out.

Rule No.82

All pupils must recite the following poem,
making a farting noise between the third
and fourth lines:

> Tarzan in the jungle
> Had a belly ache
> Can't find the toilet...
> Whoops, too late

Rule No.86

Go up to a swot and say, 'Antidisestablishment-
arianism is a very long word. Can you spell it?'
As soon as they attempt to, give them a dead arm
and say, 'Wrong! 'It' is spelled I T.'

Rule No.84

If you drink a whole bottle of cider to get your
courage up before playing spin the bottle, you
must throw up into someone's mouth.

RULE NO.85

Before giving your end-of-term report to your parents, you must change all the Es to Bs.

RULE NO.83

If someone brings in a fancy new Tupperware lunchbox, you should check to see if it's really airtight by farting in it just before lunch.

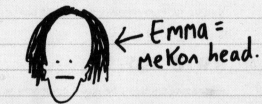

← Emma = Mekon head.

RULE NO.87

If a thick kid tries to impress you by doing a rubbish magic trick, like that one where it looks as if your thumb is moving up and down your hand, pretend to be really impressed, like you can't work out how they're doing it, and you think it's real magic.

RULE NO.88

When sitting next to someone you hate, stretch your arm round and tap them on the opposite shoulder from where you're sitting, so they look around and see that nobody's there.

RULE NO.89

If a poor kid drops 10p on the floor, say, 'Careful, you've just dropped your dad's wages on the floor.'

RULE NO.90

If someone you hate falls over, you must go up to them and ask, 'Are you alright?' If they answer 'yes', you should give them a dead arm and ask, 'What about now?'

RULE NO.91

You must scare gullible first-years by telling them the corridor on the top floor is haunted by a girl who died 50 years ago, and that you can see her face if you look in the mirror at midnight. You should also tell them that you contacted her using a ouija board, and she said she was coming to get them.

RULE NO.92

When everyone is standing in line and waiting for their medical, you should tell the gullible kids that the nurse has got a massive jar of Vaseline and she's going to give everyone a full anal probe.

RULE NO.93

All pupils must change the words to TV themes to make them ruder, as with 'Popeye the Sailor Man':

> I'm Popeye the Sailor Man
>
> I live in a caravan
>
> And when it gets chilly
>
> I play with my willy
>
> I'm Popeye the Sailor Man

RULE NO.94

You must try and shine the reflection of your watch into the headmaster's face during assembly.

RULE NO.95

When the English teacher laughs at the comedy bits of a Shakespeare video, you must look at him like he's a mong. The only bit you should laugh at is when one of the actors says the word, 'Bastard'.

RULE NO.96

All parents must tell their kids that bullies are cowards, and if you stand up to them, they'll stop picking on you.

RULE NO.97

All kids told rule no.96 must come home the next day with their faces mashed in, as the bully in question i

Things You Must Do If Someone Calls Your Mum A Prostitute Who Does It For 50p A Go

- Pour a can of drink down the front of their trousers/skirt and tell everyone that they've pissed themselves.

- Empty the contents of their bag into a toilet.

- Say that their dad's a rent boy.

- Hide all their stuff in your locker and pretend you don't know where it went.

- Tell everyone that you saw them wearing their PE kit at the weekend because it's the only clothes they've got except for their school uniform.

not actually a coward, but a dangerous psychopath who will be in prison a couple of years after leaving school.

rule no.98

If the teacher is giving out felt tips, do not touch the brown one. It is the poo pen.

rule no.99

You should ask your friends if they've seen a BMW. If they say 'yes', you must tell them that it stands for 'Black Man's Willy'.

rule no.100

If you catch the school dorks thinking up anagrams, reciting Monty Python sketches, talking Elvish, or making colour-coded revision notes, you should give them beats.

rule no.101

The only French words that you should learn on your exchange trip are 'merde', 'encule' and 'putain'.

RULE NO.102

Never lend your ruler to a pupil who's too poor to afford one themselves. They'll put fleas on it.

RULE NO.103

Before entering the examination hall, deny having done any revision, even if you're a complete swot and everyone knows it.

RULE NO.104

If you see someone panicking before entering the exam hall, you should tell them that their entire future rests on the result of the exam, and if they fail, they won't be able to get a job and they'll have to let gays bum them for money.

RULE NO.105

You must find out your teacher's christian name and shout it out when their back is turned.

Rule No. 106

All pupils must learn and sing the following song:

School dinners

School dinners

Concrete chips

Concrete chips

Soggy semolina

Soggy semolina

I feel sick

Toilet quick

It's too late

Done it on my plate

Rule No. 107

When bitching about a pupil you hate, you should tell everyone that their parents make them go to bed at eight o'clock, and that they're only allowed to watch 'Top of the Pops' if they brush their teeth and change into their pyjamas first.

RULE NO.108

If a pupil moves to your school from a more rural area, call them 'Sheepshagger' and pretend they admitted to you that they shagged their mum.

RULE NO.109

Always spread rumours about the teachers you hate being gay. You must also fail to realize the friendly Music teacher with the moustache really is gay.

RULE NO.110

If someone accuses you of trumping, you should say 'Smelt it, dealt it'. At which point they should say 'Said the rhyme, committed the crime'.

RULE NO.111

All boys should claim to have a girlfriend who goes to another school. They should say that she's really fit, but that they don't have a picture of her.

RULE NO. 112

If the school bully teases you, resist any comebacks you think of. So, if he walks past your gang and says, 'What's this? A gay club?' resist saying, 'No, but if it was, you'd join.' And if he says, 'Why are you so poor?' resist saying, 'Because your mum charges too much for blowjobs.'

RULE NO. 113

All weedy kids must go on about how they're learning karate, and soon they'll be able to get revenge on the school bully by killing him with their bare hands.

RULE NO. 114

If you discover on parent's evening that one of your friends has got really old parents, you should ask them why their gran and granddad came. You should also say, 'Look, it's your mum', if you see a picture of a skeleton in a textbook.

RULE NO. 115

Always make up playground games based on what was on TV the night before, like 'The Young Ones', 'Knight Rider', 'The A Team', or 'The Kenny Everett Video Show'. Even if the only thing on TV the night before was extended news coverage of a disaster, you should make up a game based on it.

RULE NO. 116

If someone has to use the school telephone, make sex noises in the background, and shout, 'Get off the phone and come back to bed.'

← Philip

← tits

RULE NO. 117

If a boy and a girl sit next to each other on the school bus, it means they love each other and they want to do it. Shout 'Oooh, stop shagging each other. Can't you wait until you get home?' at them.

Rule No.118

Everyone should start clapping and cheering when the pupil with the nervous stammer has to read something out in class.

Rule No.119

Alter the words of 'We Three Kings' as follows:

We three kings of Orient are

One in a taxi

One in a car

One on a scooter

Beeping his hooter

Following yonder star

Rule No.120

On the last day of term, all pupils are allowed to bring in toys and board games. If anyone bring in Barbie dolls, draw nipples, pubes and underarm hairs on them with a felt tip.

RULE NO.121

When making up with someone you've had a fight with, you should pretend to pat him on the back, while actually Sellotaping on a sign that reads, 'Oh yes, I like bumming'.

RULE NO.122

If you are left alone with the badge-making machine in a Design lesson, you should make badges saying, 'John is a gaylord', 'Mr Jenkins is a Joey' and 'Mandy gives out BJs at all times'.

RULE NO.123

You must tell the class div that the fittest girl in school will show him her tits for a quid.

RULE NO.124

If the fittest girl in your school actually does show the div her tits for a quid, beat him up.

Compulsory Practical Jokes

- Shove paper towels in the sinks and flood the loos.
- Put a plastic shit on your friend's desk and pretend it's real.
- Put a real shit on your friend's desk and pretend it's plastic.
- Put superglue into locker keyholes.
- Write a rude message about your teacher in shaving foam on the playing field.
- Put laxatives in the school dinners and 'out of order' signs on all the toilets.
- Bring in a Dictaphone, record everyone slagging each other off behind their backs, and then play it to the people they were talking about.
- Fill your mouth with cream of vegetable soup and pretend to be sick.
- Pour Coke into people's lockers through the holes in the top of them.

- Put cellophane over the toilets so everyone's piss goes on the floor.
- Tie someone's shoelaces together under the desk.
- Put a sign that says 'Please use other door' on all the doors.

RULE NO. 125

If someone in your class gets cussed, you should chant, 'Shame' at them until they retaliate.

RULE NO. 126

Claim to have put a piece of dog shit on an enemy's doorstep and set fire to it, causing them to get shit all over their shoes when they stamped it out.

RULE NO.127

You must also claim to have stuffed a potato in the exhaust pipe of a car, causing it to explode when the engine was turned on.

RULE NO.128

If one of your friends claims to have done any of the above things, you should rub your chin and shout 'Jimmy Hill' or 'Chinny Reckon'.

RULE NO.129

When the fat whackers are plodding around the track on sports day, everybody should clap, cheer, and sing the following song to the 'Batman' theme:

Dinner dinner

Dinner dinner

Dinner dinner

Dinner dinner

Fatman

RULE NO.130

You must tell pupils that they've got something on their tie, and then flick them on the face when they look down.

RULE NO.131

Grab the class spazmo's locker key off him and throw it in the deep end of the swimming pool.

RULE NO.132

If you fancy someone from your class write, 'I think U R fit. Will U go out with me?' on a piece of paper and ask one of your friends to hand it to them.

RULE NO.133

If one of your friends gives you a piece of paper which reads, 'I think U R fit. Will U go out with me?' and asks you to hand it to the person they fancy, you should read it out in front of the whole class.

RULE NO. 134

The swimming baths are public places, so you must act like a responsible adult. So walk through the roped-off area, climb up the ladder, and do a massive dive-bomb from the highest board.

RULE NO. 135

If there are waterslides at your pool, tell the gullible kids that people stick razors on the inside of them using chewing gum, and if you slide down them, you'll get cut open. You should also tell the gullible kids that there's a special dye in the swimming baths that makes your piss show up green, so everyone knows you're weeing.

RULE NO. 136

Point to the 'No Heavy Petting' sign at the side of the swimming pool and say to the class bum chums, 'Hard luck, guys. You'll have to wait until later.'

RULE NO.137

When leaving or entering the school site, walk slowly down the street side-by-side in gangs of four or five, so nobody can get past.

RULE NO.138

When sitting on a train or bus, put your bag on the seat next to you, so no one can sit there.

RULE NO.139

Anyone who is told to stand facing the wall until the bell goes as a punishment should wrap their arms around themselves and wriggle up and down, so it looks like they're kissing and cuddling someone.

RULE NO.140

If someone tells you the statistic that one in seven men are gay, gather five friends and find someone to pick on. You should tell them to choose between them being gay or one of you being gay. Give them beats whichever option they choose. If they say that your use of statistics is mathematically inaccurate, give them double beats.

RULe NO.141

In the school elections, vote for the cool kid whose manifesto is longer breaktimes and shorter detentions, and not for the swot whose manifesto is apples in the tuckshop, a voluntary litter patrol and more vegetarian options at lunchtimes.

RULe NO.142

You are forbidden to leave the school grounds during free study periods. However, if you climb over the fence on the side that isn't overlooked by the staffroom window, you should be able to make it down to the shopping precinct, where you can get tramps to buy cigs and cider for you.

RULE NO. 143

You must recite the following poem:

Beans, beans

Good for your heart

The more you eat

The more you fart

The more you fart

The better you feel

So let's have beans

For every meal

RULE NO. 144

If someone crawls between your legs to release you in a game of Stuck in the Mud, you must hold them there and fart in their face.

RULE NO. 145

If a pupil makes an accidental farting noise by rubbing their shoes together, opening a creaky door,

or dragging their textbook across their desk, shout,
'You eggy bastard' at them, and pretend it stinks.
If they deny it, it only proves they supplied it.

RULE NO. 146
Always snigger when you hear any of the following
words or phrases: masticate, pianist, free period,
seamen, homo sapiens, organism, Uranus, Christopher
Lillycrap, Shaggy, 'BJ and the Bear'.

RULE NO. 147
If you manage to sneak a look inside the out-of-
bounds sixth-form common room, you should tell
everyone that you saw them having a sex orgy.

RULE NO. 148
If you end up sitting next to a really lush girl in class,
slowly put your hand further and further
up her leg, and ask her if she's nervous yet.

Things You Must Tease
Poor Kids About

- They've got nits because they can't afford shampoo.

- Their parents give them tins of food for Christmas.

- They back their exercise books with old wallpaper, because they can't afford magazines.

- They eat 5p crisps because they can't afford Griddles or Outer Spacers.

- They eat 'value' biscuits because they can't afford Trios, Yo-Yos or Breakaways.

- They wear plain black pumps in PE, because they can't afford trainers.

- They buy their bog roll from Oxfam.

- They get half a pence pocket money.

- They wear massive school uniforms handed down from older brothers and sisters.

- They're so poor they can't afford to flush the toilet in their house until it's totally full.

- When the school holds a jumble sale, their parents are always the first ones in, looking for bargains.

- They drink 'Panda Pops' because they can't afford Coke.
- Their parents get them rip-off versions of He-Man and My Little Pony from the market.
- They get free dinner tickets.
- They sell their dinner tickets for half price outside the lunch hall.
- Their glasses have been mended with Sellotape.
- Their bags are just branded 'Sports', so they Tippex the logos of cooler brands on them.
- You see them driving round with their dad at the weekend, looking for bits of scrap metal.
- They find a 1p on the floor and buy a single Fruit Salad or Black Jack from the newsagents with it. (Please note: You must check to see if the poor kid isn't one of those really hard ones from the council estate before teasing them about these things.)

Rule No.149

If you see a form in 'Just Seventeen' that you can send off for a free starter pack of tampons, fill it in with the name and address of a boy from your class.

Rule No.150

When you get your first girlfriend, you should suddenly go all mature. You can do this by painting a CND logo on your rucksack with Tippex.

Rule No.151

If a boy you hate brings in 'Smash Hits', you should find a poster of a boy-band hunk, and stick the pages together with Pritt Stick. You should then show it to everyone and say it proves he's gay.

+ BED
- CLOTHES
÷ LEGS
× AND MULTIPLY

Rule No.152

If you are persistently causing trouble with your friend, you will be forced to sit apart in the classroom. Spend the rest of the lesson turning round to look at each other and bursting out laughing.

Rule No.153

You should hold out your hand as if to shake it with a friend, and then pull it away at the last minute. Then put your thumb on your nose, and wiggle your fingers up and down.

Rule No.154

You should change the words of charity records to tease poor kids, as with 'Do They Know It's Christmas?':

Feed your mum

Let her know it's Giro time

RULE NO.155

If your class have to go to a museum to look at the preserved remains of a bronze-age man, you should say to the class spazmo, 'Hey, you didn't tell me your mum was going to be here.'

RULE NO.156

If a girl fancies a boy from another class, she should put make-up on, hang around near him while he is talking to his friend, and go red if he glances at her.

RULE NO.157

When the teacher shows you a selection of birth-control devices during the sex education lesson, steal one of the condoms. You should then fill it up

with water and drop it out of the top-floor
window or stretch it to see how large it will
go and say, 'I'm just checking it'll fit.'

RULE NO.158

As soon as the class spazmo starts using a cool bit
of slang, like boss, skill or rated, you should say
that it went out years ago, and stop using it.

RULE NO.159

If your parents ask you how school was when you
get home, you should say, 'Alright.' If they ask you
what lessons you had, you should shrug your
shoulders and say, 'Dunno.'

RULE NO.160

If the class spazmo joins in a game of Simon Says,
you must say, 'Simon says give (name of class
spazmo) a dead leg.'

Rule No.161

If a smelly pupil tries to join your group of friends, say, 'Oooh, what's that smell? Has somebody trumped?' and check the bottom of your shoes for dog shit.

Rule No.162

If the school pleb comes up to you when you're drinking Thunderbird behind the tree on the side not overlooked by the staffroom window, you should pretend to offer him some, and say, 'Do you fancy coming on a bender?' If he agrees, pull the bottle away and say, 'Eeuurrgggh! He said he wants to come on a bender. That means he's a poof.'

Rule No.163

All girls must pretend to like the class swot when they want to get the answers off him, but they must completely ignore him when he approaches them at the school disco.

Rule No. 164

When defacing the girls' toilets sign, remove the letters 'o', 'l', and 'e' from the word 'toilets'.

Rule No. 165

All boys should tell their mates they shagged the French assistant everyone fancies, but they can't tell anyone about it because she'd lose her job.

Rule No. 166

Mum insults should be changed from time to time, to keep them topical:

'Your mum's Davros.'

'Your mum's Skeletor.'

'Your mum's Mr Bronson.'

'Your mum's Mrs Mangel.'

Mike getting bummed →

oh, don't stop. I like it

RULE NO.167

The class spazmo must hang around with the dinner-ladies all lunch break, to avoid getting beaten up.

RULE NO.168

If you're picking on someone but can't think of any insults, wind them up by just repeating what they say. This will end up with them saying, 'Stop repeating what I say,' and you saying, 'Stop repeating what I say.'

RULE NO.169

You must write 'You've just pissed on your shoes' on the floor below the urinal.

RULE NO.170

If you see a gullible first-year waiting outside the sick room, you should tell him that if he feels ill, it's probably because his periods are starting.

Embarrassing Things That Must Happen To You

- Your younger brother or sister starts school, and they tag along with you, even though you've told them not even to look at you if they see you with your friends.

- Your mum drops you off right outside the school gates and insists on kissing you goodbye while everyone watches.

- Your mum invites the school's biggest geek to your birthday party without asking you.

- You get chosen last when the teams are picked in PE.

- Your mum attaches your mittens to your coat with elastic.

- You sing 'Listen to this, too good to miss' to get everyone's attention, and no fart comes out.

- You sing 'Listen to this, too good to miss' and follow through.

- You organize a sex orgy on the playing fields after school, but only other boys turn up.

- You admit to liking a song you didn't realize was gay, like 'Smalltown Boy' by Bronski Beat.
- A first-year gets a crush on you and starts following you around.
- The PE teacher tells you to lift the vaulting horse into the middle of the gym, and it's so heavy you fart by mistake.
- Your parents make you take your passport on the school trip, because they think Wales is abroad.

✳ RULE NO.171

If the class spazmo tries to join your gang when you're smoking behind the trees at the back of the playground, you should ask him if he wants to have a fag. If he says 'yes' say, 'Eeeuuurgggh – he wants to have a fag. That means he's gay.' As he starts to walk away, you can repeat this by saying, 'No seriously mate, do you fancy a poof?'

✳ RULE NO.172

When playing tag, always try and tag the fat kids, as they won't be able to catch up with anyone, and they'll have to be 'It' for the rest of playtime.

✳ RULE NO.173

Do not go to the same bus stop as the boys from your class who are rumoured to be gay. It is the bumming bus stop. You should wait at the next stop down the road instead.

RULE NO.174

If you manage to grab a friend's sicknote before they hand it in, you should throw it in the urinal and piss on it, to see if they fish it out.

RULE NO.175

If you see a plastic crab in the museum gift shop, you should throw it at the class spazmo and say, 'Oooh, you've got crabs.'

RULE NO.176

You must recite the following poem, while pointing to the appropriate bits of your body:

> Milk, milk, lemonade
>
> Round the corner
>
> Chocolate's made

RULE NO.177

On the map of Britain on the wall of the Geography room, you should always cross out 'Es', 'Sus' and 'Middle' from Essex, Sussex and Middlesex.

RULE NO.178

You should also cross out 'S' and 'horpe' from 'Scunthorpe'.

RULE NO.179

If someone has a food or a Tippex stain on their pants, you should point to it and say, 'Oooh, you could at least have waited until you got home.'

RULE NO.180

Go up to the pupil you hate and tell them to do an impression of a spaz. After they've been doing it for a while, you should say, 'Go on then, start doing your impression. Oh you already were? I couldn't tell.'

Ray's girlfriend →

RULE NO. 181

If you get dumped by someone in your school, you must rush around the school telling everyone that you dumped them first.

RULE NO. 182

Anybody caught reading a dictionary will be given a dead arm. Unless they were using it to look up rude words.

RULE NO. 183

If you are given a burning splint in a Science lesson, you should try and light your farts before realizing it's too difficult and giving up.

RULE NO. 184

If you have a massive spot, you should either squeeze it at someone you hate, cover your face in concealer, or run off to the bogs straight away to pop it (like having a trickle of blood running down your face looks any nicer than having spots).

RULE NO. 185

You must go up to the class spazmo, lift up their hand, start hitting them with it and say, 'Stop hitting yourself. Why are you hitting yourself?'

RULE NO. 186

If someone tells you you've got B.O. you should tell them to fuck off and pretend you don't care. Then go to the toilets and spray half a can of deodorant on your underarms.

RULE NO. 187

If you see a tramp hanging around outside the railings of the playground, you should run up to a pupil you hate and say, 'Your dad's outside and he wants to speak to you urgently.'

RULE NO. 188

All pupils must learn and sing the following song:

> Bum tit tit
>
> Bum tit tit
>
> Play the willy banjo
>
> Bum tit tit
>
> Bum tit tit
>
> Play the fanny organ

Neil's drink →

RULE NO. 189

During Maths lessons, you must type the number 5318008 into your calculator, and turn it upside down.

rule No.190

If you leave your packed lunch in your locker over the weekend by mistake, you should open it and release the pong next to the school slapper. Then tell her to close her legs.

rule No.191

If the class pleb has to run between bases in rounders, you should do an impression of them running like a spastic.

rule No.192

When they get into the fifth-form, all boys must grow bumfluff moustaches so they can get cigs from the newsagent, get into 18-rated films and buy 1.5 litre bottles of cider at the off-licence.

Lee 4 Boy George

RULE NO.193

If a pupil tells a dirty joke, you must laugh at it whether it's funny or not, to prove that you understand it.

RULE NO.194

If a teacher has an unusual hairstyle, such as a comb-over, you must try and brush your hair into that style before entering the classroom.

RULE NO.195

If somebody drops a plate in the school cafeteria, everyone should clap and cheer.

RULE NO.196

If someone grasses you up to a dinnerlady for hitting them, say they hit you first, so the dinnerlady can't be bothered working out what actually went on.

Dares

You must admit who you fancy, or act out one of the
following dares:

- Bring in a screwdriver and unscrew everything in
  the classroom.
- Tell the ugliest girl in the class that you think she's
  really fit.
- Make loud shagging noises in assembly.
- Tell the school bully that he only picks on people
  because he's really gay and if he lets you bum him
  he'll feel a lot better about himself.
- Piss in the staffroom kettle.
- Knock on the door of the headmaster's office and run
  away.
- Touch a hot tripod in a science lesson.
- Rub a ballpoint pen into the groove of your ruler
  until it's hot, then give yourself a tattoo with it.

← paul and mike = bum chums

RULE NO.197

If a copy of 'Emmanuel' is doing the rounds at your school, you must try and borrow it, even though all the good bits have been worn down because the tape's been paused too much.

RULE NO.198

If one of your friends claims to have a new girlfriend, you must either say, 'Oh yeah, she's the one with the sunglasses and the white stick,' or 'Where is she now, then? Locked in her kennel?'

RULE NO.199

If you witness an accident in the playground, you must exaggerate it when telling everyone about it, like there was blood everywhere, and the ambulance men had to take someone away on a stretcher.

RULE NO.200

All pupils must learn and sing the following song:

Build a bonfire, build a bonfire

Put the teachers on top

Put (name of teacher) in the middle

And burn the fucking lot

RULE NO.201

If you have to sit next to a pupil you hate, wait until it goes quiet and shout, 'No, I don't think the teacher's a twat and I'm surprised you even said it.'

Sam Fox is 100% fit

RULE NO.202

If any of the toilet cubicles contain bog roll, unravel it by throwing it out of a top-floor window.

RULE NO.203

If a pupil you hate tries to make friends with you,
you should say, 'What was that? I thought I heard
something,' whenever they speak.

RULE NO.204

If a fifth-year girl leaves her bag unattended,
you must try and steal her birth-control pills,
so you can make your friends eat them as a dare.

RULE NO.205

Drop a 10p coin into a urinal and wait to see if any
kids are gyppo enough to actually pick it out.

RULE NO.206

If one of your friends is off sick, you should start
the rumour that he broke his arm by wanking too
hard, or that he had to go to a burns unit after
trying to shag a melon that he put in the microwave.

RULE NO.207

If the whole class have to take turns to read out a poem, everyone should start laughing when it's the turn of the boy whose voice is breaking.

RULE NO.208

Do impressions of any pupils with speech impediments such as lisps, after they've read out loud.

RULE NO.209

All girls must say, 'I'll show you mine if you show me yours' to boys. If they do, wiggle your little finger at them rather than dropping your pants.

RULE NO.210

If your friend writes their name on all their stuff, always try to make it rude by adding letters or crossing them out. For example, add 'P' before 'Rick', add 't' after 'Ben' and cross out the 'Y' in 'Gary.'

RULE NO. 211

All pupils must learn and sing the following song:

Hitler has only got one ball

The other is in the Albert Hall

His mother, the dirty bugger

Cut it off when he was small

RULE NO. 212

If the newsagents has a sign up saying that only one schoolkid is allowed in at once, everyone should take their ties off and pretend they're adults.

RULE NO. 213

You must do a 5... 4... 3... 2... 1 countdown along to the clock on the 'Programmes for schools and colleges continue shortly' screen, and cheer when the programme comes on.

Ray
4
tracey

Rule No. 214

If one of your friends gets caught stealing from the newsagents and has to go in the back room for questioning, you should spread the rumour that he was caught stealing gay porn.

Rule No. 215

You should spend the school day-trip to Calais buying firecrackers, or looking for groceries with rude names, like a drink called 'Pschitt', a chocolate bar called 'Big Nuts', or an ice cream called 'Bum Bum'.

Rule No. 216

If a teacher reveals they have a hobby, such as motorbikes, spend the whole lesson asking them questions about it, to get out of being taught anything.

Robert's mum is a bitch

RULE NO. 217

When the career-guidance officer asks boys what they want to do, they must all answer either 'gynaecologist' or 'porn star'.

RULE NO. 218

When filling in your career-guidance form, you'll be asked to enter your name, date of birth and sex at the top. Write 'Yes, please' next to 'Sex'.

RULE NO. 219

When bibles are handed out in assembly, you must search through the Book of Revelations to try and find the bit about Damien from 'The Omen'.

RULE NO. 220

If a girl in your class has facial hair, draw biro moustaches on yourself, or hold a comb under your nose and say, 'Look, this is you.'

Rumours You Must Spread
About The Kid You Hate:

- You caught him sniffing the seat of the fittest girl in school.

- He can't ride his bike without stabilizers.

- He has to go to the toilet sitting down, like a girl.

- Milk comes out of his nipple.

- He can't wee without pooing at the same time.

- He's got a mild form of Down's syndrome, but they let him go to a normal school because all the special ones were full.

- He asked for a Salter's Science kit for his birthday.

- If he hears a loud noise such as an ambulance, he has an eppy and starts battering whoever's next to him, even if it's his mum.

- Nobody asked him to come to the school disco, so he stayed in and had a disco of his own – with his parents.

- He practises snogging on his sister.

- His mum cuts his hair using a pudding bowl.

- His mum caught him having a wank.

- He invited everyone in the school to his birthday party, but nobody went.

- He has to pay everyone in his gang 50p a day just to hang around with him.
- He won't go in the school showers without his swimming trunks on.
- His mum's so fat she can't buy normal clothes and has to wear a smock.
- His balls haven't dropped yet.
- He's not allowed to watch 'Dr Who' because he poos his pants when the Cybermen come on.

RULE NO. 221

If two boys get sent out of class, they should do a bumming mime outside the classroom window.

RULE NO. 222

Always make spastic faces through the window if you see someone getting told off in a classroom at lunchtime.

RULE NO. 223

Get to school early in winter, so you can skid on the icy patches on the playground before the caretaker turns up and covers them with sand.

RULE NO. 224

You must keep asking questions in class to delay the bit of the lesson where your teacher tells you to turn to your textbooks and start working. For example: 'Miss, is a fart a gas?'

'Miss, are there any gay animals?'

'Miss, if someone's got ginger hair, does it mean they're deformed?'

RULE NO.225

If the Science teacher leaves you unguarded in the lab, you should either have Bunsen-burner fights, or mix together all the chemicals you can find, to see if it creates an explosion.

RULE NO.226

When picking on someone, you should hold them in a headlock and ask them questions like, 'United or City?', 'The Pistols or The Clash?' 'Nike or Adidas?' You should give them beats whichever option they choose.

RULE NO.227

If the dinnerlady tells you off for picking on the school mong, and says, 'Now, have you got something to say to him?' you must say, 'Yeah, fuck off.'

RULE NO.228

You must go up to the pupil you hate and say, 'Gimme Five', then pull your hands away at the last minute, so they end up whacking their hands on the desk.

RULE NO.229

If the class spazmo tries to hang around with you, send them off to the canteen to buy you a Coke, and then move to another bit of the playground.

RULE NO.230

If one of your friends bends down to tie their shoelace, put your crotch in their face and say, 'Why are you trying to give me a BJ? Why are you so gay?'

RULE NO. 231

If your friend is concentrating on his work, you can get him to admit embarrassing things by saying, 'You know when you piss in the bath?' If he absent-mindedly says, 'Yeah?' you should run around telling everyone he pisses in the bath.

RULE NO. 232

If you forget to bring in your PE kit, you must either wear something from the teacher's lice-ridden stash of spare clothes, or do it in your undies and get nicknamed 'Skid Marks.'

RULE NO. 233

Always try and modify your uniform to the game you're playing. If you're playing Superman, put the hood of your coat over your head, and leave the rest of it to dangle like a cape, and if you're playing The Karate Kid, fasten your tie around your head.

RULe NO.234

If your dad lets you watch an 18-rated video he rented from the shop, you should tell everyone it was brilliant, even if it was 'Deathwish 3', 'The Howling 4', or 'No Retreat, No Surrender 2'.

RULe NO.235

If someone from your class has the same name as a character in a film or TV show, you should say their name in the style of it. For example, you should say 'Elllllliot' like ET, and 'Ro-land' like Janet off 'Grange Hill'.

RULe NO.236

You must recite the following poem:

Liar Liar

Pants on fire

Your hair's sticking up

Like a telephone wire

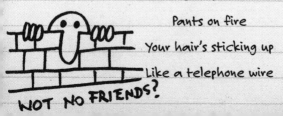

NOT NO FRIENDS?

RULE NO. 237

If you see a boy with trousers that are too short for him, shout 'Half-mast' at him.

RULE NO. 238

Always say 'It's the Fonz' when combing your hair.

RULE NO. 239

If you break friends with someone, you should tell everyone all the secrets they've told you, like that they fancy Mandy from 5B, their middle name is Roderick, and that they pissed the bed after they saw 'Jaws'.

RULE NO. 240

If one of your friends comes in wearing a new ski jacket, tracksuit top or pair of trainers, you should either say, 'They went out years ago' or pretend you saw it down the market for £10.

RULE NO.241

If someone grasses you up to a dinnerlady for calling them gay, say that you thought gay meant happy and weren't aware of any other meanings.

RULE NO.242

You must ask the shortest boy in your class if he knows that wanking stunts your growth.

RULE NO.243

Anyone caught reading in the library at lunchtime instead of playing British Bulldog should be given a wedgie, a Chinese burn or a dead leg.

RULE NO.244

However, if you're forced to spend time in the library due to teacher strikes, or turning up too late for the swimming bus, you should pass time by reading the sex bit in 'Forever' by Judy Blume.

RULE NO. 245

Girls who choose subjects like Metalwork, Physics, and Design and Technology in their options are lesbians.

RULE NO. 246

If a pupil from your school has a serious accident, you must wait until at least a couple of hours after the announcement before making jokes about it.

RULE NO. 247

If you find a large plastic bottle, you should fill it with water and wait in a toilet cubicle. Then, when someone comes in, you can pretend to be having a really long piss, complete with sighs of relief.

RULE NO. 248

When putting chewing gum in someone's hair, try to cover as much of it as possible, so a huge chunk will have to be cut out by the teacher.

The Rules of PE Lessons

- Every boy and male teacher in the school should cram into the sports hall on the day the fifth-form girls have their trampoline lesson.

- You must throw the undies of the last person to get out of the showers down the corridor.

- You must try and set off the fire alarm when the fifth-form girls are in the showers, to see if they all run out naked.

- When playing tennis, boys should stuff two balls down the front of their T-shirt and say, 'Look – this is you,' to the girl in the class with big tits.

- If the PE teacher leaves you unattended, everyone should try and throw balls at the class spazmo while he runs around the gym.

- You should wait until you get into the swimming pool to take your loose plasters off.

- In football, you should always put fat kids in goal, as they're so fat they'll fill up the entire space between the posts.

RUle NO. 249

All pupils must learn and sing the following song:

Yum, yum, bubblegum

Stick it up your mother's bum

When it's brown, pull it down

Yum, yum, bubblegum

RUle NO. 250

If you bring in a whoopee cushion, you should hide it under your coat, let it off when you walk past teachers, and look at them like they've just farted.

RUle NO. 251

If you put a whoopee cushion on the teacher's chair, everyone in the class must laugh so much when the teacher walks in that they check their chair before sitting down and confiscate it.

RULE NO. 252

On the coach to the swimming pool, everyone should sing, 'Stop the coach, I need a wee wee' to the tune of 'Glory, glory, hallelujah'.

RULE NO. 253

All boys should flick the last person to get out of the shower with their towels, until somebody points out that it looks a bit gay.

RULE NO. 254

If the class pleb slips over on a cross-country run and gets mud on the back of his shorts, you must shout 'Eeeuurgghh! Look at his skidmarks.'

RULE NO. 255

If the school geeks put a list on the notice board to see who wants to join their role-playing games club, put the names of all the kids you hate on it.

RULE NO. 256

If the school bullies are about to get you, suggest
a new trick to play on the class spazmo, like getting
him to drink a bottle of lemonade that everyone
has pissed in, so the bullies go and do that instead.

RULE NO. 257

If you want to carve out your tag on the desk
during a lesson, you must sit directly behind a fat
Jabba, so the teacher can't see what you're doing.

RULE NO. 258

When scaring gullible first-years, you should tell
them that the hardest school kids in the area
are coming round for a fight after school.

Rule No.259

And tell them that the hardest kid in that school wants to fight them personally.

Rule No.260

If your friend gets a stiffy on the school bus, tell everyone that it's because he fancies the boy sitting on the back seat, and he wants to bum him.

Rule No.261

If someone gives you a dead arm, you should pretend it didn't hurt and say, 'No effect.' You should then go round the corner and rub your arm.

Rule No.262

If you decide to make friends with someone, you should recite the following poem:

> Make friends, make friends
> Never, never break friends

If you do

You'll catch the flu

And that will be the end of you

RULE NO. 263

If a first-year's pet has just died, tell them that it will be inside the spam fritters at lunchtime.

RULE NO. 264

When queuing, slap the person in front of you on the back of the head, and say, 'Pass it on.' If the slaps gets to the weedy kid standing behind the school bully, and he won't do it, give him a dead leg.

RULE NO. 265

When entering the classroom, you should always try and get a seat at the back of the class. You should then lean back on your chair so that only two legs are on the floor.

RULE NO.266

If a girl who is rumoured to stuff her bra with tissues walks past you in the corridor, shout 'Kleenex' at her, and blow your nose really noisily.

RULE NO.267

No matter how badly you need a poo, you must wait until you get home to do it, because anyone who sits down on the school toilets will get AIDS.

RULE NO.268

If you've got the squits and you have to use the school toilets, cover the seat with toilet paper. AIDS can't pass through toilet paper.

RULE NO.269

If you're hanging around with your gang, you should beckon the class spazmo over to you. When he says, 'What?' you should say, 'Fuck off.' You should repeat

this until he doesn't come over anymore, at which
point you should beat him up for disobeying you.

RULE NO. 270

If your whole gang is getting told off by the headmaster, you should snigger at anything that sounds
even a bit rude. This will set everyone off laughing,
and make the headmaster even more angry.

RULE NO. 271

You must throw a 2p piece at a pupil you hate and say,
'Here's the money I owe your mum for last night.'

RULE NO. 272

You must call your friend a
'dickfer' and when they ask,
'What's a dickfer?' you must
say, 'Aaaah! Don't you know
what a dick's for?.'

RULE NO.273

If someone in your class brings in a briefcase, you should call them 'Briefcase Boy' and draw a willy on it with a Tippex pen.

RULE NO.274

If someone in your class comes in wearing a blazer, you should call him 'Blazer Boy' and write 'Shag me here' on the back of it, with an arrow pointing down to his arse.

RULE NO.275

You must learn and sing the following song:

Georgie Best

Superstar

Looks like a woman

Wears a bra

Things Teachers Must Say

- I don't care who started it.

- Are you chewing? Into my hand, now.

- Something's obviously very funny, so why don't you share it with the rest of us?

- Concentrate – I've no intention of going through all of this again.

- You won't find the answer written on the ceiling.

- What have you seen out of the window that's so interesting?

- This is for your benefit, so please wake up.

- Do you know how much it costs for the caretaker to remove graffiti?

- Honestly, it's like talking to a brick wall sometimes.

- I'd expect that kind of behaviour from him, but really, I'm surprised at you.

- If you're so clever, why don't you come up here and take the lesson?

- Concentrate, class. I'm not saying all this for the good of my health.
- Last night's homework did not make for happy reading.
- Would you do that at home?
- I don't mind staying back after class. I've got lots of homework to mark.
- Oh, thank you for gracing us all with your presence.
- Give me one good reason why I shouldn't give you a detention.
- Perhaps you'd like to tell the rest of the class what I just said.
- Come on, we're waiting.

Kung Fu

RUIE NO.276

If a kid you hate walks up to you when you're with your gang, make him paranoid by saying, 'Anyway, we better stop talking about him now – he's here.'

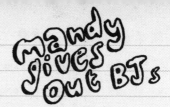
Mandy gives out BJs

RULE NO. 277

You must ask a friend if he thinks he's special. If he answers 'yes', you should say that this means he's supposed to go to a special school, which means he's a spaz.

RULE NO. 278

If there's a kid in your class who stinks of shit because he never washes, everyone should trap him in a circle and spray their deodorant cans on him.

RULE NO. 279

If a boy from your class holds a ruler in front of his crotch and says, 'Look, here's my willy,' you should get the wooden metre ruler from the blackboard and say, 'Look, here's mine.'

RULE NO. 280

If the school bully starts walking with a limp because he thinks it makes him look hard, do not point out that it actually makes him look mildly spastic.

⭐ RULE NO. 281

If your friend won't show you the porno mag he's brought in, you should say, 'Yeah, well, some of us don't need porno mags, because we've got the real thing.' You should then fish around in his bag for it when he's not looking.

RULE NO. 282

When you come into school after falling off your bike, and everyone wants to know what caused all your cuts and bruises, you should say, 'I got into a fight last night. You should see the other guy, though. He's in hospital!'

RULE NO. 283

You must put your friend in a headlock and tell him he has to choose between being a gay and shagging the ugliest girl in the class. If he chooses shagging the ugliest girl in the class, you should run off to tell her he wants to shag her.

RULE NO. 284

If a pupil you hate is about to sit down, pull their chair away, so they fall backwards.

RULE NO. 285

When the teacher's taking register, you should burp the words, 'Here, miss.'

C.P.

T.C.

RULE NO. 286

If your friend does a fart which you actually quite enjoy the smell of, you must never admit it to him. That would be really gay.

Rule No.287

If you ever have to wait for anything, like the bus
to the swimming pool, you should sing:

> Why are we waiting?
>
> We are suffocating

Rule No.288

You must tell the gullible first-years that a
crocodile lives in the sewers, and if they use the
school toilets it'll jump up and bite their knob off.

Rule No.289

If a kid admits that certain noises go through them,
like the scraping of metal on dinner plates or the
grinding of school jumpers between teeth, you should
keep making this noise near them.

Rule No.290

If a thick kid tries to make friends with you by

telling a rubbish joke, get everyone to pretend it's really funny so he keeps on telling it.

RULE NO. 291

If your friend has to go and see the headmaster, but he won't tell you why, spread the rumour that he was caught wanking in the stockroom.

RULE NO. 292

If you need money, you should wait in a corridor and charge the div kids 10p to get past. If any of them hand over the money, you should say, 'It's 20p tomorrow.'

RULE NO. 293

If the school boffin gives a presentation in front of the class or goes up to collect his Chess trophy in assembly, everyone should do spastic clapping when they're supposed to applaud.

RULE NO.294

You should never sit on the chair that the pupil you hate has just sat on. It is the gay chair.

RULE NO.295

If someone from your class comes up with a money-making scheme, like Gonch off 'Grange Hill', try to spoil it for him. For example, if they bring in a multipack of chocolate bars to sell individually, leave their bag on the radiator so they all melt.

→ RULE NO.296

If a girl blows you out when you ask her to go to the pictures with you, you should tell everyone that she's frigid, and keep shouting, 'Close your legs, it's cold' at her.

RULE NO.297

If a boy out of your class is rumoured to be a

gaylord, you should get changed as far away from him as possible after PE, and say, 'Make sure you don't bend down near him.'

RULE NO. 298

If one of the cool kids gives you a drag of the spliff they're smoking behind the trees that are not overlooked by the staffroom window, start talking in an American accent, and pretend to be hallucinating.

RULE NO. 299

If the class flid tries to shake hands with you, you must crush his hand in a death grip until he goes on his knees and begs to be released.

RULE NO. 300

If the class Joey tells you the name of his favourite TV programme, change it to something rude to tease him, like The Gay Team and The Littlest Homo.

Rule No.301

If a boy and a girl sit next to each other, you should sing the following song at them:

(Boy's name) and (girl's name)

Sitting in a tree

K - I - S - S - I - N - G

First comes love

Then comes marriage

Then comes (girl's name) with a baby carriage

Rule No.302

Catch out your friends by asking them if they've done a sex act that doesn't actually exist.

Rule No.303

If a boy who has a name that can also be a girl's name, such as Sam, Joe or Vic, speaks to you, say, 'Is she trying to speak to me? I can't understand what she's saying. I don't speak girl language.'

Your Body: The Facts

- Girls' tits are made out of milk.

- If you don't fart, the gas will build up inside you and you'll die.

- If you keep your eyes open while sneezing, they'll pop out.

- Girls wee out of their arses because they don't have knobs.

- If you sneeze and fart at the same time, you'll explode.

- Throughout your whole life, your head never changes size.

- If you swallow chewing gum, you'll die.

← Kate

RULE NO.304

Before pushing someone over, you should get one of your friends to crouch down behind them first, or ask them if they've stepped in dog shit so they check the bottom of their shoe.

 ← Mark's dad.

RULE NO.305

Rather than throwing litter away, you should hand it to a friend and say, 'You touched it last. It's your litter now.'

RULE NO.306

All pupils should cheer when the fire alarm goes off.

RULE NO.307

All pupils with ginger hair should be called 'Carrot', 'Ginner', 'Ginger Nut' or 'Ginger Minger.'

RULE NO.308

All pupils with curly hair should be called 'Pube Head', all pupils with a centre parting should be called 'Fanny Parting' and all pupils with large sideburns should be called 'Mutton Chops'.

RULE NO.309

Say to someone, 'Say when,' then start moving your fingers apart. If the other person says 'when' when the gap's small, say, 'Ding dong ding dong, your knob's this long.' If the gap's large, say, 'Ding dong ding dong, my knob's this long.'

RULE NO.310

If you're left unattended in the Music room, don't bother trying to play something from the stack of LPs that the teacher keeps in the corner. The only remotely recent thing in there is an album of disco cover versions of classical music.

RULE NO.311

If the class spazmo falls over during PE, shout,
'All pile on!' and jump on top of them.

RULE NO.312

If you see a boy and a girl sitting next to each
other, you must sing the following song:

> Oh dear, what can the matter be?
>
> (boy's name) and (girl's name)
>
> got stuck in the lavatory
>
> They were there from Monday to Saturday
>
> Nobody knew they were there

RULE NO.313

When it's harvest time, you
will be asked to bring in
spare groceries and tins to
give to disadvantaged families
in the local area. On the morning of collection,

ooh, come
on buy it!
only 10p

←Tracey from 5

hand your tins straight to the poorest kid in the class and say you're cutting out the middle man.

RULE NO. 314

If two boys have a fight because they both fancy the same girl, the girl should pretend to be upset and tell them to stop fighting. Later, the boys should make friends while they're waiting to be told off by the headmaster and agree she's a prick tease.

RULE NO. 315

If the bring-and-buy sale poster says, 'All proceeds go to charity', you should replace the word charity with the name of the poorest kid in your school.

RULE NO. 316

Girls must refuse to accept that the pop stars they fancy in 'Look-In', 'Tops', 'Number One' and 'Smash Hits', are very clearly gay.

RULE NO. 317

If a secret post service is created for Valentine's Day, everyone should send an anonymous card to the school minger, saying she's really fit and they want to go all the way with her.

RULE NO. 318

If you don't have any genuine hickies to show off, make them on your neck with a bicycle pump.

RULE NO. 319

All boys should spend the day before the school disco covering themselves with deodorant and spraying their mouths with breath-freshener.

RULE NO. 320

At the school disco, the boys must line up on one side of the hall, and the girls must line up on the other side, waiting for the first person to start dancing.

RULE NO.321

While you're waiting, you should say to your friends, 'This place is dead. Should we go to a nightclub instead?' before deciding to stick around and see if it picks up.

RULE NO.322

If your friends ask you why you're not chatting up the girl you fancy, you must say, 'Slowly slowly catchy monkey' and change the subject.

RULE NO.323

When you get the courage to approach a girl, try a line like, 'Hi, I'm Mr Right. Somebody said you were looking for me', 'Do you believe in love at first sight, or shall I walk by again?' or 'You must be very tired, because you've been running through my mind all night.' Then stand around in an embarrassed silence trying to think of something else to say.

Rule No.324

If a girl blows you out at the school disco, tell your friends she's obviously a lezza, you didn't fancy her when she started speaking, or that it's not your fault she was giving out all the signals.

Rule No.325

After getting off with a girl at the school disco, you should walk her to the bus stop, kiss her goodbye and tell her you had a lovely night. You should then run back to your mates and show off by holding out your middle finger for them to smell.

Rule No.326

Any boys who fail to cop off should start fighting each other at the end of the night, like they're too hard to be interested in girls anyway.

RULE NO.327

All boys must spend the day after the school disco
boasting about how they had it off with a girl,
even though all they actually did was snog her.

RULE NO.328

All boys who don't manage to get off with anyone
should pretend that they pulled a really fit girl
who came down from another school, but they
can't remember her name.

RULE NO.329

You must recite the following poem when dipping to
see who's going to be 'It' in a game of tag:

Ip dip doo

Doggy does a poo

Cat does a wee wee

Out goes you

← Tracey

hairy pits

Sex: The Facts

- Wanking makes you blind.

- Kissing with tongues makes you pregnant.

- The only other way girls can get pregnant is if a boy sticks his finger in their belly button.

- Sometimes girls do blowjobs. They do this by putting a man's willy in their mouths and blowing.

- Gays do sex with each other by bumming. They do this by rubbing their bums together.

- If you're still a virgin by the time everyone else in your class says they've done it, you're frigid.

- The average size of the male penis is between 15 and 25 inches. You have absolutely nothing to worry about if yours is between these lengths.

- A wet dream is when you piss the bed.

- If you wank too much, your knob will fall off.

- AIDS was started when a bloke shagged a monkey.

- All men who sit with their legs crossed are gay.

RULE NO.330

All pupils must snigger and do a bumming mime if a teacher says, 'I'll deal with you after the lesson.'

RULE NO.331

All pupils, whatever their age, must pretend to have seen the following films: 'The Exorcist', 'I Spit on Your Grave', 'Driller Killer', 'Evil Dead', 'The Texas Chainsaw Massacre', 'Debbie Does Dallas', 'Deep Throat', and anything with King Dong or John Holmes in.

RULE NO.332

When choosing GCSE options, take into account which subjects the fittest girls are doing, which have the softest teachers, and which sound most like a doss, e.g. Sports Science and Child Care.

RULE NO.333

All teachers have no idea how to turn the TV to the video channel. They should try and do it themselves for ten minutes, before going off to fetch one of the Science lab assistants.

RULE NO.334

All boys should pull both pockets out of their trousers and say to girls, 'Do you want to see my elephant impression?'

RULE NO.335

All pupils must sing the following song:

> What do you do if you need to have a poo
>
> In an English country garden?
>
> Pull down your pants and poo on all the plants
>
> In an English country garden

i am a spac.
signed
Ray.

Rule No.336

You must ask your friends if they know that spunk floats in the bath. If they say yes, run around telling everyone that they wank in the bath and that they're a dirty bastard.

Rule No.337

If one of your friends is wearing a pair of trousers which are too big for him, you should either tell everyone that he's wearing flares because he doesn't know they've gone out, or say that he pooed his trousers and had to get a replacement pair from the dinnerlady's stash of spare clothes.

Rule No.338

If your friends ask you if you love the girl you've been snogging, you should say, 'Nah, she's just another notch on the bedpost.' You should completely deny having said this if it gets back to her.

RULE NO. 339

Towards the end of the fifth year, teachers should give up on showing Science and Maths videos to Set Four, and start showing them educational dramas about what it's like to be jobless, and the demands of being a single mum.

RULE NO. 340

Don't bother pretending to be ill so you can stay at home and watch TV. All they show is programmes for schools and colleges.

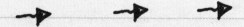

RULE NO. 341

Everyone must boo when the teacher pauses the educational video and says, 'Now, let's all write down the facts we've just learned.'

RULe NO.342

You must trick the class divs by asking them things like, if they've seen a film called 'Spastics say No.'

Dan shagging his dog.

RULe NO.343

If you get a high score while playing Chuckie Egg on the school BBC B, you should enter your name as 'Keith is a poof.'

RULe NO.344

If the class spazmo tries to join in when you're playing on the BBC B, you should tell him that his mum said he's not allowed to play in case he gets too excited and has an eppy.

A Glossary for Younger Readers:

Opal Fruits – Starburst

Marathon – Snickers

First year – Year Seven

Fifth year – Year Eleven

BBC B – Playstation 2

Video – DVD

Look-In – Sugar

Chuckie Egg – GTA Vice City

Porno mag – Porn site

Sam Fox – Jordan

A mexican pissing in a bucket.